Fact Finders™

Questions and Answers: Countries

Turkey

A Question and Answer Book

by Mary Englar

Consultant:
Sabri Sayari
Director, Institute of Turkish Studies
Georgetown University
Washington, D.C.

Capstone
press

Mankato, Minnesota

Fact Finders is published by Capstone Press,
151 Good Counsel Drive, P.O. Box 669, Mankato, Minnesota 56002.
www.capstonepress.com

Library of Congress Cataloging-in-Publication Data
Englar, Mary.
  Turkey : a question and answer book / by Mary Englar.
  p. cm.—(Fact finders. Questions and answers. Countries)
  Includes bibliographical references and index.
  ISBN 0-7368-3762-0 (hardcover)
  1. Turkey—Juvenile literature. I. Title. II. Series.
DR417.4.E54 2005
956.1—dc22   2004018997

Summary: Describes the geography, history, economy, and culture of Turkey in a
question-and-answer format.

Editorial Credits
Rebecca Glaser, editor; Kia Adams, series designer; Kate Opseth, book designer;
  Nancy Steers, map illustrator; Wanda Winch, photo researcher; Scott Thoms, photo editor

Photo Credits
Atlas, 12–13, 18–19; Cuneyt Oguztuzun, 4, 15, 25; Fatih Pinar, 21
Aurora/laif/Murat Tueremis, 17
Coral Planet/Izzet Keribar, cover (background), 11, 12; Mehmet Gulbiz, 9, 18, 22–23
Corbis/Dave Bartuff, 27; Owen Franken, cover (foreground)
Getty Images Inc./Hulton Archive, 7
Photo courtesy of Richard Sutherland, 29 (bill)
Photo courtesy of Worldwide Bi-Metal Collectors Club/Joel Anderson, 29 (coins)
StockHaus Ltd., 29 (flag)
Woodfin Camp & Associates, Inc./Robert Frerck, 1

Artistic Effects
Photodisc/Jonelle Weaver, 24; Siede Preis, 16

1 2 3 4 5 6 10 09 08 07 06 05

Table of Contents

Features

Where is Turkey?

Turkey lies in both Europe and Asia. The Asian part of Turkey is called Anatolia. A small sea separates European Turkey from Anatolia. Turkey is a little larger than Texas.

Turkey's landforms change by region. European Turkey and western Anatolia are lowlands with forests and plains. About half of Turkey's crops are grown there.

Turkey's highest mountain, Mount Ararat, forms part of the eastern border. ➤

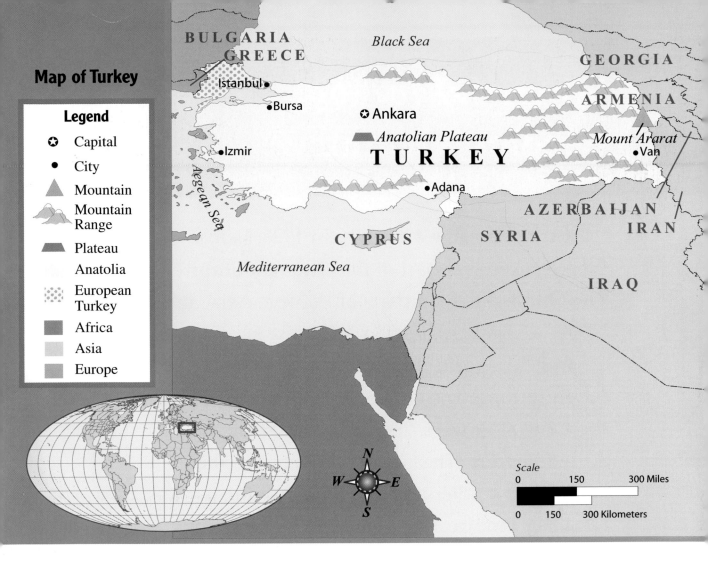

Anatolia is bordered on three sides by seas. The hot, sunny coasts have good farmland. Central Anatolia is a dry **plateau**. High mountains cover eastern Turkey. Mount Ararat is the tallest point. Winters are snowy in the mountains and in central Turkey.

When did Turkey become a country?

Turkey became a country in 1923. Before then, Turkey was part of the Ottoman **Empire**. The Ottomans ruled parts of Europe, Asia, and North Africa from 1300 to 1922.

In 1914, World War I (1914–1918) broke out in Europe. The Ottoman Empire joined the **Central Powers**. They fought against the **Allied Powers**. The Central Powers lost the war. Allied soldiers tried to break up the Ottoman Empire. They invaded Turkey.

Fact!

Kemal Atatürk was born as Mustafa Kemal. In 1935, the Turkish National Assembly gave him the name Atatürk. It means "father of the Turks."

Kemal Atatürk founded Turkey in 1923. He led the country until his death in 1938.

Turks were upset with the Ottoman government because it could not defend Turkey. Kemal Atatürk united the Turks and other groups. The Turkish army drove out the Allied soldiers in 1922. On October 29, 1923, Atatürk formed the Republic of Turkey.

What type of government does Turkey have?

Turkey's government is a parliamentary democracy. In this system, people vote for **representatives** in **parliament.**

Turkey's parliament is called the Turkish Grand National Assembly. Its 550 representatives make laws. The assembly elects a new president every seven years. The president represents Turkey at world meetings. The president can also turn down laws.

Fact!

Turkish presidents can only serve one seven-year term. They cannot be reelected.

The Turkish Grand National Assembly meets in Ankara, the capital of Turkey.

The president chooses a **prime minister** to run the government. The prime minister chooses the Council of Ministers. The council is similar to the U.S. cabinet. The ministers are in charge of government departments, such as defense and education.

What kind of housing does Turkey have?

Most people in Turkish cities live in apartments. In the suburbs, some people have small houses. Turkish cities are very old. New apartment buildings are sometimes built next to old shops and **mosques**. More than half of the people in Turkey live in large cities.

Where do people in Turkey live?

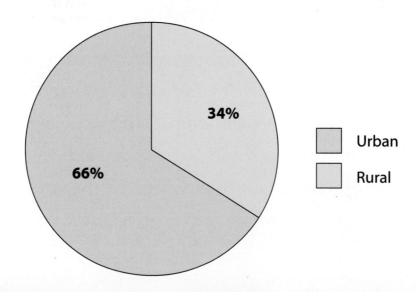

34%

66%

Urban

Rural

High-rise apartment buildings share the sky with mosques in Istanbul.

Outside cities, housing is made with materials from the area. Forests provide wood for houses near the Black Sea. In east-central Turkey, people use dirt and water to make mud-brick houses.

What are Turkey's forms of transportation?

Turkey has modern roads and railroads. In large cities, the roads are very busy. Many people ride taxis and buses to work. Some cities have light-rail lines.

Ferries cross the water every few minutes between Istanbul and Anatolia. Many people travel to work by ferry.

People ride ferries to cross the sea between Anatolia and European Turkey. ➤

Most Turks travel by taxi or bus. Some travel by light-rail train.

Turks travel around the country by airplane or bus. Airlines fly to and from large cities. The bus is cheaper and easier for most Turks. Turks travel between small towns by bus.

What are Turkey's major industries?

About 40 percent of Turks work as farmers. They grow cotton, fruit, olives, nuts, and grain. In the central plateau, many Turks raise sheep and cattle. Extra food is sold to other countries.

Another 40 percent of Turks hold service jobs. These jobs include teaching, banking, and tourism. Tourists come to see Turkey's historic buildings and to enjoy the beaches.

What does Turkey import and export?	
Imports	*Exports*
chemicals	clothing
machinery	fruit and nuts
oil	textiles

Farmers grow olives near the Aegean Sea.

The other 20 percent of Turks work in factory jobs or mining. Factory workers make clothing, **textiles**, and steel. Turkey mines its natural resources of coal, copper, and iron.

What is school like in Turkey?

Primary school in Turkey lasts for eight years. Most children start school at age 7. School is free, but students must pay for their uniforms, books, and supplies. The schools are crowded. Some students can go to school only in the morning or only in the afternoon.

After primary school, students choose a high school. General high schools prepare students for universities. Students learn job skills at technical schools.

Fact!

In primary schools, students have the same teacher from first through fifth grades.

Some Turkish schools require students to wear uniforms.

To attend universities, high school students must take an entrance test. If they pass, students pay only a small fee to attend.

What are Turkey's favorite sports and games?

The most popular sport is soccer, which Turks call *futbol*. Children play soccer in the streets when they have free time. Turks cheer for their pro soccer teams.

The Turkish government encourages people to play sports. In addition to soccer, Turks like basketball, volleyball, swimming, and wrestling.

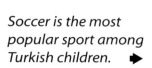

Soccer is the most popular sport among Turkish children. ➤

In greased wrestling, olive oil makes wrestlers' skin very slippery.

One unusual wrestling tournament is held every summer. It is called greased wrestling. The wrestlers cover themselves with olive oil. Their skin becomes slippery. It is difficult to hold on to another wrestler.

What are the traditional art forms in Turkey?

Turkey has long been known for its beautiful carpets. Explorer Marco Polo wrote about the beauty of Turkish carpets 800 years ago. Carpets cover cold floors in homes and mosques.

The best carpets are woven by hand. No two carpets are the same. The weavers are usually women and girls. A handmade carpet may take several years to finish.

Fact!

Turkish writer Orhan Pamuk writes novels about life in Turkey, especially Istanbul. His books are now famous worldwide.

Turkey is famous for its handwoven carpets.

The traditional Turkish art of tile painting began during the Ottoman Empire. Handpainted tiles were used in mosques, palaces, and government buildings. Today, handpainted tiles are still made in the Kutahya **province** in western Anatolia.

What major holidays do people in Turkey celebrate?

Turks celebrate National Independence and Children's Day on April 23. On this day in 1920, the first Grand National Assembly met in Ankara. Atatürk later added Children's Day to the holiday. He wanted to honor children because they are important to Turkey's future.

Almost all Turks are **Muslims**. Each year, Muslims fast for 30 days. They do not eat between sunrise and sunset. In Turkey, this month is called Ramazan.

What other holidays do people in Turkey celebrate?

Kurban Bayrami
National Republic Day
New Year's Day
Victory Day
Youth and Sports Day

Children from different countries are invited to Turkey to celebrate Children's Day.

At the end of Ramazan, the Turks celebrate Seker Bayrami, or Sugar Festival. Turks clean their houses and buy new clothes. They prepare food for their visitors. Families get together, give gifts, and eat candy and sweets.

What are the traditional foods of Turkey?

Turkish dinners often begin with several small appetizers called mezes. Common mezes are olives, cheese, stuffed grape or cabbage leaves, or vegetable salads. Lamb or fish and rice are served next. Bread is served with every meal. Many Turks finish their meals with fresh fruit. Some people have sweet pastry desserts like baklava. Tea or Turkish coffee is served after every meal.

Fact!

Tea is the national drink of Turkey. Turks drink 160,000 tons (145,152 metric tons) of black tea each year. That is more than the weight of 20,000 African elephants.

Grapes are grown in the Black Sea region.

Many of Turkey's popular foods are produced in the country. Sheep farmers provide lamb meat. Fish and seafood are caught near the coasts. Grapes, cherries, peaches, oranges, and melons are all grown in Turkey.

What is family life like in Turkey?

In the cities, most families are made up of parents and their children. Grandparents may also live with them. Many mothers work outside the home. In poor families, children work when they are not in school.

What are the ethnic backgrounds of people in Turkey?

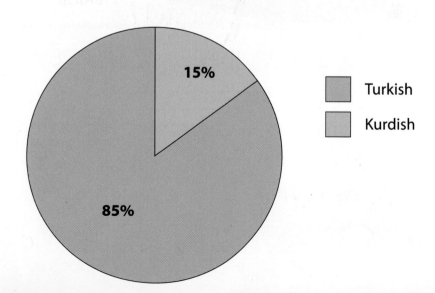

Turkish

Kurdish

Turks enjoy spending time with their family.

In small towns, larger family groups live together. Grandparents, aunts, or uncles may live with a family. Young adults stay with their families until they get married. In farming families, every member of the family works in the fields when needed.

Turkey Fast Facts

Official name:

Republic of Turkey

Land area:

297,590 square miles
(770,760 square kilometers)

Average annual rainfall:

15 inches (38 centimeters)

**Average
January temperature:**

32 degrees Fahrenheit
(0 degrees Celsius)

**Average
July temperature:**

73 degrees Fahrenheit
(23 degrees Celsius)

Population:

71,325,000 people

Capital city:

Ankara

Languages:

Turkish, Kurdish

Natural resources:

antimony, borate, chromium,
coal, copper, hydropower,
iron ore, mercury, sulfur

Religions:

Islamic   99.8%
Christian, Jewish   0.2%

Money and Flag

Money:

Turkish money is called the lira. In 2004, 1 U.S. dollar equaled 1,326,095 liras. One Canadian dollar equaled 999,629 liras.

Flag:

The Turkish flag has a white crescent and star on a red background. The color red represents the blood of Turks who fought for independence. The star and crescent are traditional Islamic symbols.

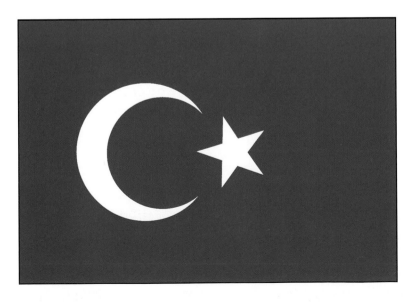

Learn to Speak Turkish

Turkish is the official language of Turkey. Learn some Turkish words using this chart.

English	Turkish	Pronunciation
hello	merhaba	(MER-hah-bah)
good-bye (person leaving)	allahaismarladik	(ah-LAH-us-mar-lah-duk)
good-bye (person staying)	güle güle	(guh-LAY guh-LAY)
please	lütfen	(LOOT-fahn)
thank you	tesekkür ederim	(tesh-uh-KUR eh-deh-rim)
yes	evet	(EH-vet)
no	hayir	(HEYE-ur)

Glossary

Allied Powers (AL-ide POU-urs)—a group of countries that fought together in World War I and won; these countries included England, France, Greece, Italy, and the United States.

Central Powers (SEN-truhl POU-urs)—a group of countries that fought together in World War I and lost; these countries included the Ottoman Empire, Germany, and Austria-Hungary.

empire (EM-pire)—a group of countries or tribes that have the same ruler

mosque (MOSK)—a building used by Muslims for worship

Muslim (MUHZ-luhm)—a person who follows the religion of Islam; Islam is a religion whose followers believe in one god, Allah, and that Muhammad is his prophet.

parliament (PAR-luh-muhnt)—the group of people who have been elected to make laws in some countries

plateau (pla-TOH)—an area of high, flat land

prime minister (PRIME MIN-uh-stur)—the person in charge of a government in some countries; Turkey's prime minister is in charge of the Council of Ministers.

province (PROV-uhnss)—a district or a region of some countries; Turkey is divided into 67 provinces.

representative (rep-ri-ZEN-tuh-tiv)—someone who is elected to speak for others in government

textile (TEK-stile)—a woven or knitted cloth

Internet Sites

FactHound offers a safe, fun way to find Internet sites related to this book. All of the sites on FactHound have been researched by our staff.

Here's how:
1. Visit *www.facthound.com*
2. Type in this special code **0736837620** for age-appropriate sites. Or enter a search word related to this book for a more general search.
3. Click on the **Fetch It** button.

FactHound will fetch the best sites for you!

Read More

Alexander, Vimala, Neriman Kemal, and Selina Kuo. *Welcome to Turkey.* Welcome to My Country. Milwaukee: Gareth Stevens, 2002.

Orr, Tamra. *Turkey.* Enchantment of the World. New York: Children's Press, 2003.

Pavlovic, Zoran. *Turkey.* Modern World Nations. Philadelphia: Chelsea House, 2004.

Sheehan, Sean. *Turkey.* Cultures of the World. New York: Marshall Cavendish, 2003.

Index